Natural Thrills

Freeskiing and Other
EXTREME SNOW SPORTS

by Elliott Smith

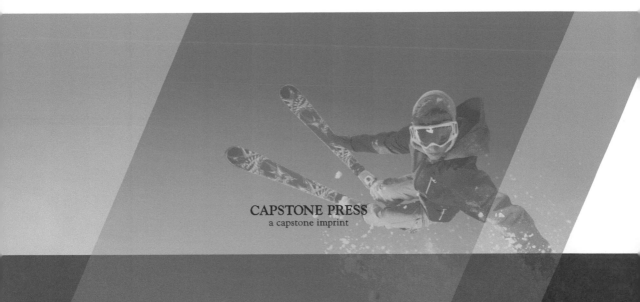

CAPSTONE PRESS
a capstone imprint

Edge Books is published by Capstone Press, an imprint of Capstone.
1710 Roe Crest Drive
North Mankato, Minnesota 56003
www.capstonepub.com

Library of Congress Cataloging-in-Publication Data is available on the Library of Congress website.
ISBN: 978-1-5435-9004-3 (hardcover)
ISBN: 978-1-4966-6609-3 (paperback)
ISBN: 978-1-5435-9008-1 (ebook pdf)

Editorial Credits
Anna Butzer, editor; Cynthia Della-Rovere, designer; Kelly Garvin, media researcher; Katy LaVigne, production specialist

Photo Credits
Associated Press/Christian Pondella/Red Bull Content Pool via AP Images, 4-5; Newscom/Andrew Wilz/Icon SMI, 25; Shutterstock: Alexander Rochau, cover, backcover, alexfe, 9, Budimir Jevtic, 28, Dmytro Vietrov, 12, gorillaimages, 27, Ipatov, 11, Leopoldo Lunghi, 21, McKerrell Photography, 23, Parilov, 17, 19, Savostin Ivan, 6, yanik88, 15

Artistic elements: Shutterstock: Artur Didyk, Dmytro Vietrov, Mumemories, Pavel Burchenko, pupsy

All internet sites appearing in back matter were available and accurate when this book was sent to press.

Printed in the United States   5559

Table of Contents

CHAPTER 1

A World of Powder

Standing at the top of a snow-covered mountain, the sound of silence is loud. The route to the bottom is straight down. But at the **apex** of some of the world's biggest peaks, freeskier Michelle Parker isn't scared. Instead, she's happy. Whether she is in the mountains of Alaska or Europe, the path she creates is her own.

Michelle Parker skis in the mountains near Mammoth Lakes, California.

"The freedom of choosing my own way down the mountain had me hooked," Parker said about freeskiing.

One of Parker's most memorable skis happened in Japan. Myoko Kogen is one of the country's oldest ski resorts. Some skiers say it is home to the best snow in the world. Parker helped create a ski film about the area, highlighting the natural beauty and tree-lined runs. She said that being in the outdoors and flying down the mountain is a unique feeling. "When you feel that when you're skiing, it does make it more of a special experience," she said.

apex—the highest point of something

CHAPTER 2

What is Freeskiing?

There's only one way down from the top of a mountain. Or is there? Freeskiing athletes are able to explore the natural **terrain** during their runs. There are no rules, no set paths, and no **gates** to follow.

Many freeskiing athletes enjoy the sport because they are able to ski freely, anywhere, any place, and on any terrain they want to ski on.

Usually, freeskiing features big, fast turns and long, steep **vertical descents**. It also features cliff drops. Freeskiing gives athletes the chance to create their own course. They can create unique **lines**, attempt jumps, or build tricks, all while flying down the slope. Freeskiing is sometimes called big mountain skiing to help separate it from freestyle skiing.

Freestyle skiing competitions are usually timed races. Skiers try to get the best time on the course. Freeskiing doesn't have a time element. It's more focused on creativity and difficulty. Freeskiing athletes enjoy the thrill of the ride. Skiers try to find less popular mountains to freeski down.

terrain—the physical features of a piece of land
gates—narrow poles with flags attached; some skiers carve around gates
vertical—straight up and down
descent—the action of moving downward, dropping, or falling
line—a path down a mountain or hill

When it comes to freeski mountains, bigger is better. Many big mountain courses are not available to **recreational** skiers because of the danger involved. Some of the best places for freeskiing include Crested Butte in Colorado and Big Sky Resort in Montana. Big Sky's course has a 4,350-foot (1,326-meter) vertical drop!

Skiing at the 2022 Olympics

While freeskiing is not an Olympic sport, there are several ski events to watch during the next Games. The freestyle events in Beijing will feature five events: moguls, halfpipe, ski cross, aerials, and ski slopestyle. All of these events feature big jumps, cool tricks, and high speeds. Some events are judged, while others are races. While the courses are not fully natural and sometimes use created snow, watching them is still a rush. U.S. athletes won three medals in the 2018 Olympics, including a gold in men's Ski Halfpipe.

recreational—relating to an activity done for enjoyment
stable—not easily moved

A freeskiing athlete hits the slopes at Big Sky Resort in Montana.

The skis used on big mountains are different from traditional skis. Most freeskis are longer and heavier than traditional skis. Athletes need to be **stable** when going fast on rough snow and steep terrain. Most freeskiers use skis that are taller than they are because the length helps with stability.

CHAPTER 3

Snowboarding

A combination of surfing, skateboarding, and skiing, snowboarding has boomed in popularity in recent years. The sport's origins date to the 1960s with the invention of the "Snurfer," a sled-like board. The board allowed riders to surf on snow. Other creators began making improvements, eventually leading to attaching ski boots to the board.

Snowboards today are high-tech creations that give athletes the ability to perform crazy tricks and tackle steep mountains. While nearly anyone can try snowboarding, only the most extreme athletes take on big mountain snowboarding. After all, going down a cliff called The Shoulder of Death seems a little scary!

What makes big mountain snowboarding so difficult is a combination of speed and control. Without ski poles to help control the body, these athletes must be masters at **maneuvering** the board. Many of the best snowboarders say their board becomes an **extension** of themselves as they rocket down mountains.

A snowboarder performs a trick called a lein, where their front hand grabs the heel edge of their board.

While most big mountain riders participate for fun, there are competitions for the top athletes. Those events are judged based on rider lines, jumps, and board control.

Tricks are a huge part of snowboarding. The Elbow Curve is a move during which a rider places one arm on the ground and spins the board. When doing a Backside 180, a rider almost completes a full rotation and then does a reverse spin at the end.

maneuver—to make planned and controlled movements that require practiced skills
extension—an addition

CHAPTER 4

Snowkiting

Most people think about kites at the beach, but in snowkiting, the fun comes to the mountains. Much like windsurfing, snowkiting uses the power of a breeze to help create an extreme ride. The sport began in Europe in the 1970s and has spread across the globe.

Athletes use large foil kites that are controlled by either two or four lines. These kites are almost like a parachute. Because the kites are soft, there is no damage when they fall to the ground. They can easily be relaunched after a crash and packed away when the day is done. Athletes pair a kite with skis or a snowboard, depending on what they **prefer**. Larger kites are harder to control but provide more power, which is why experts use them.

prefer—to like one thing better than another

While snowkiting can take place anywhere there's snow and wind, advanced athletes can bring their gear to the mountains. There, the wind allows them to go both up, down, and even sideways along the slope. Depending on the wind and terrain, snowkiters can soar in the air as the kite pulls them upward. Because snow is usually a pretty smooth surface, not much wind is needed to get started with a snowkite.

Snowkiting can be done on mountains or big hills, but flat ground is even more ideal.

The world's toughest snowkiting race, Ragnarok, is an 80-mile (129-kilometer), five-lap marathon. Only a handful of the racers finish in the five-hour time frame. Racers must dodge other kites, **slalom** through rocks, and battle difficult wind conditions to succeed.

slalom—a downhill race in which riders weave through sets of poles

CHAPTER 5

Ski Biking

Another combination of two sports, ski biking gives riders a unique way to ride down the slopes. On the surface, the idea seems simple. Remove the wheels from a bike frame and attach a pair of skis. Once riders are ready, they attach a pair of short skis to their feet and hit the trail! Ski biking is sometimes called skibobbing to help separate it from regular biking. The first ski bikes date back to the 1800s, where they helped **transport** goods through mountains.

transport—to move or carry something or someone from one place to another

The learning curve for ski biking is much easier than regular skiing. So, if riding a bike comes naturally, this might be a way to start on the mountain. And unlike skiing, ski biking is gentle on a skier's knees. Some big mountain areas are making room for ski bikes as the sport continues to grow.

Ski biking is growing in popularity around the globe.

Ski bikes can be expensive to purchase, but some resorts offer rental bikes that can be used. In addition, there are kits that upgrade old bikes into ski bikes for a fraction of the price.

Professional ski bikers take part in races, located mostly in Europe. The speed record on a ski bike is 125 miles per hour (201 km per hour), set during a race in France in 2003.

Fat Tire Biking

Fat tire biking is another way to get rolling on the snow. Riders who use their mountain bikes to explore trails in the summer were tired of being stuck in the winter. So, they came up with a unique solution. Athletes replaced the bike's normal tires with oversized tires that featured maximum **traction**. The tires are usually between 4 to 5 inches (10 to 12.7 centimeters) wide. This gives riders the ability to pedal through the snow and uphill without slipping. The Fat Bike World Championships is a 25-mile (40-km) cross-country race held in Colorado where riders tackle all types of terrain.

Fat tire bikes allow biking enthusiasts to get their wheels turning no matter the weather conditions.

traction—the amount of grip one surface has while moving over another surface

CHAPTER 6

Snocross

The high-speed sport of snocross brings the power of engines to fresh powder for thrilling competitions. Snocross features snowmobiles zooming through natural courses, where athletes must pull off jumps and make tight turns. The sport developed from motocross, which shares many of the same characteristics as the snow event.

The machines used in snocross, usually called sleds, are very powerful. The weight of an average sled is 460 pounds (210 kilograms). They can reach heights of up to 100 feet (30 m) coming off ramps.

Snocross races are intense. Riders battle for position while soaring over jumps and other **obstacles**.

Snocross is gaining popularity in the United States. Events such as the X Games and the Snocross Series Tour draw big crowds. Snocross athletes have played a role in this growth by hosting youth clinics. These events give young riders an opportunity to learn how to improve both on and off the track.

obstacle—an object or barrier that competitors must avoid during a race

CHAPTER 7

How to Get Started

Michelle Parker is one of the few women who participates in big mountain freeskiing. She wants to help create awareness of the sport and get more girls and women involved. That's why she makes ski films of her adventures down some of the world's toughest mountains.

"The next generation of women needs strong role models, and I want to be that," says Parker.

Skiing and other snow sports are a great way to experience winter fun. However, it is important for beginners to make safety and training a priority before hitting the slopes.

The first step is to have all the proper equipment with the right size and fit. Beginner skis and snowboards should be short and flexible. This makes them easier to turn and control. Boots should be flexible so knees go over the toes. All bindings should be checked by a ski technician. And a helmet that fits properly is a must. Winter sports athletes should always dress warmly.

Beginners should practice stopping safely and controlling their speed at all times.

Many ski resorts and snowboard parks have **certified** instructors who can help teach beginners important first steps. Learning from a pro can make the process easier and more fun. Practicing on the bunny slope or smallest ramp can help solidify the right moves. Always practice with a parent or instructor nearby. As a bonus, many resorts offer free beginning lessons to first-time skiers.

The elite athletes in extreme freeskiing and snowboarding have been on the slopes since they were very young. It takes years of practice and training to attempt any extreme ski, jump, or race. Snow sports participants should always be aware of potential dangers. Some dangers include weather, obstacles, and other skiers or boarders. Being safe on the slopes can keep everyone out of trouble.

Getting out in the snow is a great way to appreciate natural beauty. Pick a snow sport, keep practicing, and get ready to have some *cool* adventures!

Being safe on the slopes includes wearing bright colors that can be easily seen by other athletes.

certified—having officially recognized training, skills, and abilities

Glossary

apex (AY-peks)—the highest point of something

certified (SUHR-tuh-fyd)—having officially recognized training, skills, and abilities

descent (di-SENT)—the action of moving downward, dropping, or falling

extension (ek-STEN-shun)—an addition

gates (GATES)—narrow poles with flags attached; some skiers carve around gates

line (LINE)—a path down a mountain or hill

maneuver (muh-NOO-ver)—to make planned and controlled movements that require practiced skills

obstacle (OB-stuh-kuhl)—an object or barrier that competitors must avoid during a race

prefer (pri-FUR)—to like one thing better than another

recreational (rek-ree-AY-shuhn-uhl)—relating to an activity done for enjoyment

slalom (SLAH-luhm)—a downhill race in which riders weave through sets of poles

stable (STAY-buhl)—not easily moved

traction (TRAK-shuhn)—the amount of grip one surface has while moving over another surface

transport (transs-PORT)—to move or carry something or someone from one place to another

terrain (tuh-RAYN)—the physical features of a piece of land

vertical (VUR-tuh-kuhl)—straight up and down

Read More

Garrison, Hal. *Snowkiting*. New York: Gareth Stevens Publishing, 2018.

Raum, Elizabeth. *Chloe Kim*. Mankato, MN: Amicus High Interest, 2018.

Whiting, Jim. *Snowboarding*. Mankato, MN: Creative Education, 2018.

Internet Sites

Expert Advice: Skiing Kids
https://www.rei.com/learn/expert-advice/skiing-kids.html

Healthy Living: Skiing and Snowboarding
https://www.healthychildren.org/English/healthy-living/sports/Pages/Skiing-and-Snowboarding.aspx

The Snow Pros: Professional Ski Instructors
http://www.thesnowpros.org/take-a-lesson/beginners-guide-to-skiing

INDEX